The Project Manager's Little Book of Assumptions

Roland McLain-Smith

The Project Manager's Little Book of Assumptions

First Published in 2011 by Roland McLain-Smith

ISBN 978-1-4466-1792-2

Version 1

FOREWORD

This book may be wrong…

ASSUMPTIONS

1   Each problem has a palatable solution just waiting to be found

2   Teams in an open plan office communicate better than teams in a closed plan office

3   The question you asked is the question you wanted to ask

4   Common sense will prevail

5   The car park ticket machine's clock is synchronised with your wristwatch

6   "Early next week" means "Monday or Tuesday next week"

7   Emails and SMS messages arrive at their destination within five minutes of being sent

8   The larger the book, the more you are likely to learn from it

9   People who confidently make an allegation will be able to back it up

10   Telepathy and Telekinesis are, at best, unproven concepts and therefore no-one on your project will expect to use them

11   An ally today is an ally tomorrow

12 The phrase "I will be going on holiday on Friday 15th August for 2 weeks" means, among other things, that the individual concerned will be unavailable on Friday 15th August

13 A day with no meetings in your diary will be a quiet day

14 No news is good news

15 Project teams fully understand the role of their project manager

16 A risk is being managed as long as it is noted in the Risk Log

17 The phrase "project plan" means a GANTT chart

18 Your email will be interpreted as you intended

19 Accurate forecasting consists of extending forward the current trajectory

20 Everyone's definition of "busy" is the same as yours

21 People will only apply the phrase "a good team" to an effective and well-managed team

If we all worked on the assumption that what is accepted as true is really true, there would be little hope of advance.

Orville Wright

22   People who are favoured, are favoured
      for good reason

23   The number of documents produced
      by a project manager is proportional to
      his/her effectiveness

24   Because it is obvious to everyone, it
      will be picked up

25   The customer's written requirements
      will explain what they want

26   It is more likely to be correct if you
      take your time over it

27 Once customer requirements are signed off, the customer will lose the desire to change their mind

28 Your team will carry their mobile phones around with them

29 My prejudices are better than yours

30 An upgraded version will be better than the version it replaces

31 Project board members know what a project expects of them

32 If you take a day off sick, it takes about an hour to catch up the following day

33   Dial 9 for an outside line

34   Suppliers who are large and established are more likely to meet your needs

35   People are committed to the success of the project and the company

36   Other people's definitions of "committed" and "success" are the same as yours

37   A supplier will remember to factor public holidays into their lead times

If you drink much from a bottle marked 'poison' it is almost certain to disagree with you, sooner or later.

A. A. Milne "Alice's Adventures in Wonderland"

38   You will get more done working from home

39   If someone's diary shows they are free at a particular time, it means they are free to meet you at that particular time

40   A person who leaves at 5pm is less committed than one who leaves at 6pm

41   A supplier can successfully lead a client to a fit-for-purpose solution if the client isn't yet sure what they want

42   It is good to have a "can do" attitude within a "can't do" culture

43   Your customer will be happy to bring planned dates forward but won't be happy with any delays

44   Pay peanuts, get monkeys

45   It is safe to abbreviate

46   A project board will not reverse a decision it previously made

47   The advice provided by the technical expert will remain valid for the duration of the project

48   People will let you know if they can't open the attachment on your email

49   A small change has a small impact. A big change has a big impact

50   Those leaving a meeting will all have the same recollection of that meeting

51   If someone sends you a document pointing out 3 changes they've made, it means those are the only changes they've made

52   If a supplier says they have the particular expertise you are looking for, it means they have the particular expertise you are looking for and you will have full access to it

53   It's good to talk

We simply assume that the way we see things is the way they really are or the way they should be. And our attitudes and behaviors grow out of these assumptions.

Stephen R Covey

54 "It's just around the corner" means "it is up to 200 metres away"

55 A senior manager will want to know all the facts before making a decision

56 The terms "close of play" and "close of business" mean 5pm

.

57 People learn after being corrected the first time

58 They will do it correctly because they have past experience of doing it

59 The definition of "next Friday" is obvious

60   Hitting the "Call Lift" button multiple times makes the Lift arrive more quickly

61   People don't book their next summer holiday until January at the earliest

62   Everyone understands what is meant by "12.00pm"

63   The technical expert assigned to your project is an expert in the field for which you need a technical expert

64   You will uncover what's missing from a supplier's proposal by reading it carefully and underlining statements

65   The project will deliver sooner if you throw more people at it

66   When someone says they've resolved an issue, it means they've resolved it to your satisfaction

67   A project board does not need to be reminded of decisions it previously made

68   People will find the question in a long email from you

69   Very little will happen on your project between Christmas and New Year

Whenever a theory appears to you as the only possible one, take this as a sign that you have neither understood the theory nor the problem which it was intended to solve.

Karl Popper

70   The budget will be signed off in time.

71   Project team members will let the project manager know

72   "I'll be there in ten minutes" means "I'll be there between nine and eleven minutes from now"

73   People take lunch at 1.00pm

74   It is daft to send an email to someone who sits next to you

75   Team members who will do anything to please the customer are great to have on your project

76   Dial zero for switchboard

77   You should feel honoured when a
      supplier asks you to be first to
      implement their amazing new solution

78   Success is defined as "on time and
      within budget"

79   A   formal   project   management
      qualification   makes   a   very   good
      project manager

80   People in your department are on your
      side

81   Work that has been agreed as out of
      scope will not come back into scope

82   "One working day" means 7 hours

83   "A day" means one working day

84   "A week" means 7 days

85   "7 days" means 5 working days.

86   "2 weeks" means 14 days

87   Working days are Monday, Tuesday, Wednesday, Thursday and Friday

The world comes to us in an endless stream of puzzle pieces that we would like to think all fit together somehow, but that in fact never do.

Sanity is not truth. Sanity is conformity to what is socially expected. Truth is sometimes in conformity, sometimes not.

Robert Pirsig

88 "This year" means the current calendar year from January 1st to December 31st inclusive

89 A date range like "20th July - 23rd July" means the 20th, 21st, 22nd and 23rd July not just the 21st and 22nd

90 A good PM should be at least as technical as the project's technical expert

91 It won't be allowed now because it wasn't allowed before

92 If you tell their manager, their manager will tell them

93 The customer is always right

94 Most situations are fundamentally black and white once you've cleared the fog

95 Someone else will look after the out-of-scope stuff

96 It's obvious

97 An empty diary indicates someone with no work to do

98 An email will arrive at its destination within 15 minutes of being sent

99   The telephones will keep working during a power cut

100   The definition of "a few" is "three"

101   "Resources" is just another word for "people"

102   You get what you pay for

103   If you were applauded for it yesterday, you will be applauded for it today

104   Implying it is as good as saying it

My aim is: to teach you to pass from a piece of disguised nonsense to something that is patent nonsense.

Ludwig Wittgenstein

105 Saying it is as good as documenting it

106 There will be some space to physically store your deliveries

107 People understand the meaning of the phrase "elapsed time"

108 People don't forget the meetings shown in their diary

109 Words are interpreted the same way by everyone

110 There are no opportunities in a recession

111 The meeting will start and finish on time

112 If you spend much of your time maintaining a risk log and an issue log, your project will be successful

113 Perfectionists are reliable

114 Staff will put the team's interests before their own

115 A good project manager keeps a risk log but not an assumption log because risks are much more important to the success of a project

116 Others have your best interests at heart

117 A technical expert should not be challenged on issues within his sphere of expertise

118 You can "switch off" in some of the meetings you've been invited to

119 People will react badly to being given more work

120 If you receive a 'read receipt', it means the recipient has read your email

If the world seems a bleaker place, it is because the world has changed.

Anon

121 If you deliver a clear instruction to someone to do something in a given timescale, they will do it in that timescale

122 The words "tomorrow" and "today" do not have to be qualified in email because recipients can see when the email was sent and will draw the correct conclusion about which day you are referring to

123 If you send an email to someone, they will never forward it to someone else if it says something the later recipient would wince at

124 When writing any emails or documents, you can't over-use pronouns

125 People who claim to remember their actions without writing them down are honest people who never miss a thing

126 "It will be possible" means "it will be possible barring earthquakes and meteor strikes"

127 People read all of the text in long emails

128 People don't read all of the text in long emails

129 All essential components to make a solution work will be included in the supplier's quotation

130 In answer to your question "why didn't you tell me that?" people will never say or imply "well you didn't ask"

131 If some team members aren't sure what was agreed, it means they were not concentrating when it was agreed

132 If someone says they haven't previously been told something, they are telling the truth

133 People can take a joke

134 Changes can be made to project scope without any prior assessment

What hadn't been realized in the literature until now is that merely to describe how severely something has been tested in the past itself embodies assumptions, even as a statement about the past.

Robert Nozick

135 You should only manage projects that you are comfortable with

136 If a form asks for a particular piece of information, you have to provide it

137 The culture of a company rarely has much of an impact on how you manage a project

138 Suppliers will deliver to promised deadlines

139 Sugar Puffs exit the packet at the same speed as Bran Flakes

140 Powerpoint is a software product, not a curse

141 A single company has a single culture

142 What seems like a great idea will turn out to be a great idea

143 It'll be alright on the night

144 Really wanting to do something is the same as having the habit for doing it

145 People at a meeting know the other people at the meeting and understand their roles as well.

146 Agile means Unstructured

147 It's good for a project manager to be passionate

148 A reasonable request will receive a reasonable response

149 People know what their own self-interest is and therefore how to correctly act on it

150 Delivering quality will be appreciated as much as delivering to time and cost

Crude classifications and false generalisations are the curse of organised life.

George Bernard Shaw

151 You can't teach an old dog new tricks

152 He sounds convincing so he must be right

153 It must be true because the experts say so

154 They will react the same way I did

155 Correlation is the same as Cause

156 Writing the minutes is not a particularly important role

157 People don't really read highlight reports

158 An email containing multiple questions will receive multiple answers carefully constructed to show which answer relates to which question

159 A supplier who is described by your organisation as "a partner" is more likely to be helpful/flexible

160 There will be someone available to do a quick, small job

161 Change is good

162 "Inappropriate" means the same as "wrong"

163 A lessons learned exercise will result in lessons being learned

164 To be an even better project manager, you need another PM qualification

165 Answering "No" to the question "Do we have process for that?" is a bad thing

166 It is useful to have an ambitious "project manager wannabe" on your team

I never attempt to make money on the stock market. I buy on the assumption that they could close the market the next day and not re-open it for five years.

Warren Buffet

167 You don't need to know the detail

168 You do need to know the detail

169 Team members think you need to know the detail

170 Going to the pub with one's colleagues doesn't aid project progress.

171 People will follow processes if they are documented

172 People who visit you at your desk won't read your screen while they are talking to you

173   It has been tested

174   It has been tested in a way that is relevant to your project

175   Testing is a formality

176   As long as the general direction and scope is clear, the detail can rarely trip up a project

177   Verbal agreement which is minuted is as good as a physical signature

178   People won't bother you at your desk if you are obviously eating your lunch and reading the newspaper

179 A team manager speaks on behalf of his/her team

180 Constraints noted at the beginning of a project are immoveable and cannot be negotiated during the lifetime of a project

181 People who refer in conversation to an organisation's policies know that such policies exist and have read them

182 Your project's budget is ring-fenced and you are the gatekeeper

183 Project team members will first escalate project issues to you and not to other people outside the project

If we are uncritical we shall always find what we want: we shall look for, and find, confirmations, and we shall look away from, and not see, whatever might be dangerous to our pet theories

Karl Popper

184 The document sent to you says exactly what the sender told you it says

185 Someone will support and maintain what the project has delivered after the project team has been disbanded

186 Customers don't exaggerate

187 Faced with a choice between covering one's back and moving the project forward, people will choose the latter

188 Your suggested amendments will be incorporated (unless you are explicitly told that they won't be)

189 Contractors are only in it for themselves. They should be hired with caution, treated with detachment, and kicked out with ease

190 A project manager doesn't need to get involved in the petty politics. S/he can leave all that to the project board

191 The Accounts department will tell you when a project-related invoice comes in

192 When someone complains that they don't seem able to get across the importance of a particular point, it is because their audience is stupid or isn't listening

193 You can get lots of work done when no-one is around

194 If he/she/they don't say it, then he/she/they aren't thinking it

195 If a statement is made independently by two people, it is true

196 The word "quality" means "robust and built to last"

197 Everyone's definition of the word "quality" is the same as yours

198 People don't have selective or faulty memories

It is undesirable to believe a proposition when there is no ground whatever for supposing it true.

Bertrand Russell

199 A person's domestic life doesn't impinge upon their performance

200 People will change their behaviour in predictable ways

201 Surfing news websites at lunchtime is acceptable

202 As long as you give your team general direction, they will fill in the detail in the right way

203 Progress will have been made by the time you get back from holiday

204 You actually said what you think you said

205 Someone who is brilliant in their chosen technical field will make a brilliant project manager

206 People will be productive during all official working hours

207 When someone says they accept a decision, it means they will work positively with the consequences of that decision

208 The person who runs a company or a department can easily be identified by looking at the organisation chart

209 Low cost equals low impact

210 If you send an email to the wrong address, you will get an email back telling you of your mistake

211 People don't get blamed in a "non-blame culture"

212 A complex issue will take considerable time to resolve

213 Highly-skilled and apparently indispensable people should be managed using a timid, walking-on-eggshells approach

Of two equivalent theories or explanations, all other things being equal, the simpler one is to be preferred.

A definition of Occam's Razor

214 People who carry the team's drinks tray are unimportant junior people

215 Someone who makes regular visits to the office drinks machine and/or toilets doesn't have enough work to do

216 Suppliers work well with each other

217 A supplier's problem is their problem alone

218 You don't get the best out of people by constantly reminding them of deadlines

219 Wealthy companies will make money readily available for projects

220 Poor organisations will be more rigorous with their business cases

221 A slight variation in a component's functionality means a slight impact on the project

222 The organisation that will support your deliverables when the project closes will happily accept that support role

223 A project initiation document and plan is written for the benefit of others

224 The project board will act as a buffer if the customer gets angry and has real issues with the direction of the project

225 Technology that large numbers of people use in their every day lives is mature and therefore stable

226 A supplier with a long history of business with your organisation will be better than a new supplier

227 Someone who looks and sounds professional, will be professional

228 You will reduce demand by charging

The criterion of simplicity is that the minimum number of assumptions be postulated

Albert Low

229 Changes will not be made without an authorised change record

230 If you explicitly ask someone to keep a piece of information confidential, they will do so

231 People are at their best in the morning

232 It is best to follow the process

233 A good project manager is a noisy & paranoid inflator of risks and issues

234 A permanent employee is more likely to stay

235 A permanent employee is more committed to the organisation/project

236 People are motivated firstly by being recognised/loved and secondly by being paid well

237 Contractors have different motivations to permanent staff

238 People who use long words are clever

239 You will only be blamed for things for which you were responsible

240 Graduates are more intelligent than non-graduates

241 Someone who is apparently always busy is indispensable

242 A busy person is an effective person

243 Younger people are more energetic; older people are more likely to see things through despite being more cynical

244 The definition of the phrase 'next week' is obvious

245 Someone known for their consistent humour cannot be serious

Every man takes the limits of his own field of vision for the limits of the world.

Arthur Schopenhauer

246 This week's most important project will be next week's most important project

247 Senior managers will make decisions that you will consider rational and logical

248 "Red-Amber-Green" status reporting will be objective

249 A person's attendance at a particular training course changes them into a qualified expert in that particular subject area

250 Lunch is for wimps

251 The phrase "By Tuesday" means "any time up to the end of Monday"

252 Communication between 2 people who sit next to each other will be better than communication between 2 people who sit several thousand miles apart

253 If it can go wrong, it will go wrong

254 There will be parking spaces for you and your team

255 People who always answer questions with a question of their own are incisive team players

256 "It can't be done" means "it is technically/physically impossible"

257 If a senior manager is mandating the project, there will be budget for it

258 An MBA makes for a good leader/manager

259 Spellchecker and grammar tools are better at spelling and grammar than you are

260 If you are worried, then you should be

261 If it is considered unlikely to happen then, in reality, it won't happen

The least questioned assumptions are often the most questionable.

Paul Broca

262 Project Board members and project teams understand the principles of risk and issue management

263 Project managers working at the same organisation will define project management terms in the same way

264 No matter what the organisation, project managers will always place equal emphasis on delivering to time, quality and budget

265 Normal working hours are 9.00am to 5.00pm with an hour for lunch

266 People will be available and working during normal working hours

267 You can get things done quicker by appealing to someone's good nature

268 It is secure if stored in a locked cupboard

269 No-one would be so foolish

270 Your project will take priority if any of your project team are also matrix-managed by another manager

271 A large part of a programme manager's role is to ask the question "Have you done it yet?"

272 If it is a risk to your project, then you as project manager should own it

273 Constraints that have been agreed cannot be negotiated away later

274 Constraints that have been assumed can be negotiated away later

275 If you carefully define the roles & responsibilities on your project, your team will just become demarcated jobs-worths

276 Only the good people leave

The fact that an opinion has been widely held is no evidence whatever that it is not utterly absurd; indeed in view of the silliness of the majority of mankind, a widespread belief is more likely to be foolish than sensible.

Bertrand Russell

277 When the email you sent to someone arrives in their inbox, it will look exactly the same as when you sent it

278 Before trying to fix something, people will first ask "Is it broken?"

279 Everyone understands what is meant by the term "belt and braces"

280 The obvious solution will be the answer

281 People will act according to their long-term interests

282 Jobs in large companies and the public sector are safe jobs

283 People will tell you if they no longer want to receive your highlight report

284 Your customer's requirements will not change

285 You have one customer and you know who they are

286 The terms and conditions of your supplier's engagement are only of passing interest to you and don't have the capacity to delay your project

287 Senior managers are not close enough to the situation - as you are – to make rational and logical decisions on the project direction

288 Annual Leave - particularly annual leave booked over the school summer holidays - cannot be cancelled

289 If you ask the question that everyone was scared of asking, people will see you as courageous

290 If an organisation uses a term from a well-known project methodology, the organisation will define that term in the same way as the project methodology

The child learns to believe a host of things. i.e. it learns to act according to these beliefs. Bit by bit there forms a system of what is believed, and in that systems some things stand unshakably fast and some are more or less liable to shift. What stands fast does so, not because it is intrinsically obvious or convincing; it is rather held fast by what lies around it.

Ludwig Wittgenstein

291 People know their own strengths and weaknesses. And so do you

292 Changing the format of project reporting templates will have an impact on project success

293 When the project closes, any remaining open issues can be closed

294 The business case is a rigorous and objective assessment of the business benefits a project will deliver

295 A package addressed to you will be delivered to you

296 A project manager needs the breadth and depth of knowledge to second-guess and overrule advice from all project team members including the technical expert

297 Received Wisdom is your friend

298 Old proverbs are true

299 Your project will become more busy (or more quiet) at a gradual rate

300 You will start living when you stop working

● ● ●

Man is a credulous animal, and must believe something; in the absence of good grounds for belief, he will be satisfied with bad ones.

Bertrand Russell

ASSUMPTIONS
ABOUT
ASSUMPTIONS

1   Assumptions are statements that no-one could object to

2   Assumptions have some evidence to support them

3   If an assumption has been identified, it can no longer bite you

4   You will be able to test the validity of an assumption

5   Only a small proportion of project risks arise from assumptions

6   If an assumption fails, it fails in a bad way

7   All assumptions are obvious, easily documented and recognised by everyone on the team

8   Assumption is just another word for risk.

9   Assumptions may cause aggravating issues but they don't have the capacity to completely derail a project

10 Once an organisation starts thinking about assumptions, it will no longer make assumptions, or assumptions about assumptions

11 Project Managers tend to capture assumptions in their risk log

Begin challenging your own assumptions.
Your assumptions are your windows on
the world. Scrub them off every once in
awhile, or the light won't come in.

Alan Alda

12   A convention is a safe assumption

13   One can tell if an assumption is minor

14   A hidden assumption is more dangerous than an acknowledged assumption

And hidden assumptions won't remain hidden for long; they will soon reveal themselves..........

* * *

The harder you fight to hold on to specific assumptions, the more likely there's gold in letting go of them.

John Seely Brown

About the Author

Roland McLain-Smith is a freelance project management consultant who has spent nearly 20 years working on projects and programmes in major UK organisations.

He is married with three daughters and his consultancy is at:

www.aramis-projects.com